The Mighty Stegosaurus

Jackie Golusky

BUMBA BOOKS™

LERNER PUBLICATIONS ◆ MINNEAPOLIS

Note to Educators

Throughout this book, you'll find critical-thinking questions. These can be used to engage young readers in thinking critically about the topic and in using the text and photos to do so.

Lerner Publications Company
An imprint of Lerner Publishing Group, Inc.
241 First Avenue North
Minneapolis, MN 55401 USA

For reading levels and more information, look up this title at www.lernerbooks.com.

Main body text set in Helvetica Textbook Com Roman.
Typeface provided by Linotype AG.

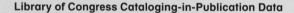

Library of Congress Cataloging-in-Publication Data

Names: Golusky, Jackie, 1996– author.
Title: The mighty stegosaurus / Jackie Golusky.
Description: Minneapolis : Lerner Publications, [2022] | Series: Bumba books - mighty dinosaurs | Includes bibliographical references and index. | Audience: Ages 4–7 | Audience: Grades K–1 | Summary: "Stegosaurus was an enormous dinosaur known for its strong tail and the plates on its back. Learn more about these plant-eating giants of North America"— Provided by publisher.
Identifiers: LCCN 2021010514 (print) | LCCN 2021010515 (ebook) | ISBN 9781728441054 (library binding) | ISBN 9781728444482 (ebook)
Subjects: LCSH: Stegosaurus—Juvenile literature.
Classification: LCC QE862.O65 G65 2022 (print) | LCC QE862.O65 (ebook) | DDC 567.915/3—dc23

LC record available at https://lccn.loc.gov/2021010514
LC ebook record available at https://lccn.loc.gov/2021010515

Manufactured in the United States of America
1-49875-49720-6/2/2021

Table of Contents

Meet Stegosaurus!

Stegosaurus lived about 150 million

years ago.

Dinosaurs are extinct. But scientists still study them.

Why do you think scientists study dinosaurs?

Stegosaurus lived mainly in North America. That's where scientists first found its fossils.

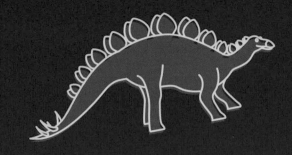

Stegosaurus was huge!

Some were 30 feet (9 m) long.

It may have used its

tail for protection.

Its front legs were shorter than its back legs. So a stegosaurus's back arched.

It had weak jaws.

It ate only plants.

What other animals eat plants?

It had plates on its back.

Scientists want to know more

about these plates.

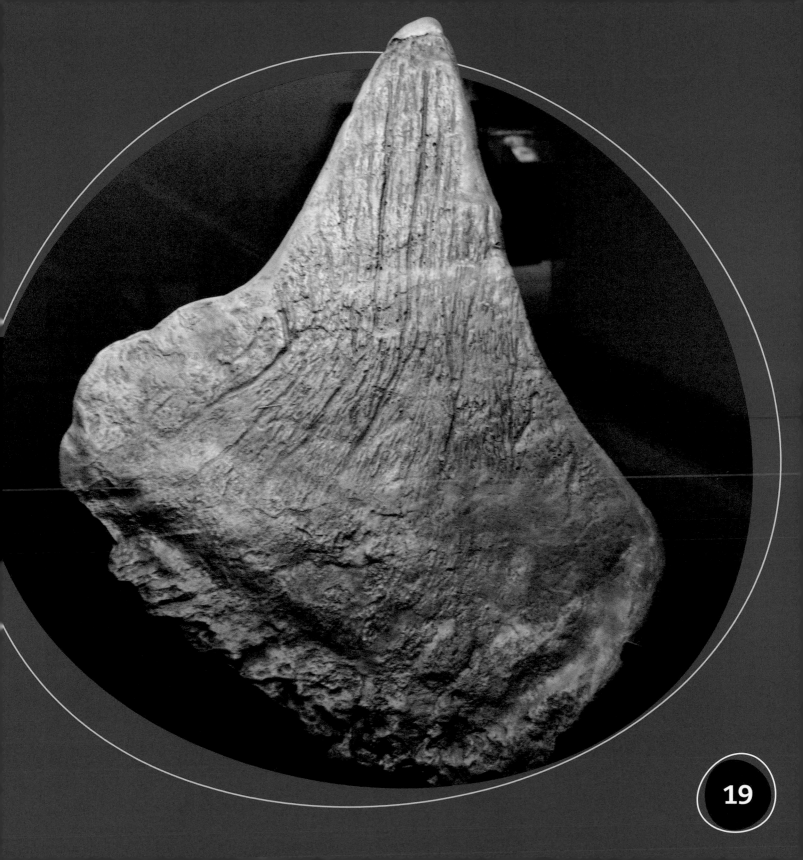

You could make the next

dinosaur discovery!

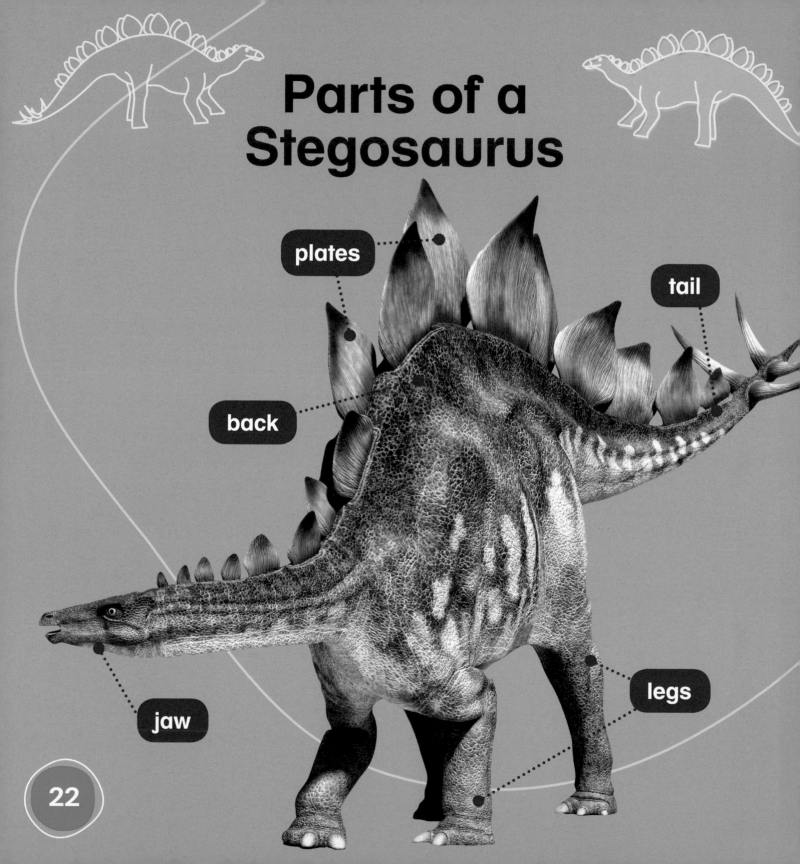

Parts of a Stegosaurus

plates

tail

back

jaw

legs

Picture Glossary

extinct

no longer alive

fossil

a trace of a living animal from a long time ago

jaw

one of the two bones where teeth grow

plate

a part that sticks up on a stegosaurus's back

Learn More

Colins, Luke. *Stegosaurus*. Mankato, MN: Black Rabbit Books, 2021.

Kaiser, Brianna. *The Mighty Brontosaurus*. Minneapolis: Lerner Publications, 2022.

Kelly, Erin Suzanne. *Dinosaurs*. New York: Children's Press, 2021.

Index

Photo Acknowledgments

Image credits: Daniel Eskridge/Getty Images, p. 5; paleontologist natural/Shutterstock.com, pp. 6, 23 (top left); Akkharat Jarusilawong/Shutterstock.com, pp. 9, 23 (top right); Daniel Eskridge/Shutterstock.com, pp. 10–11; Corey Ford/Stocktrek Images/Getty Images, p. 13; Elenarts/Shutterstock.com, p. 15; Elena Duvernay/Stocktrek Images/Getty Images, pp. 16–17, 23 (bottom left); Tim Evanson/Wikimedia Commons (CC 2.0), pp. 19, 23 (bottom right); whyframestudio/Getty Images, p. 20; Leonello Calvetti/Getty Images, p. 22.

Cover: Warpaint/Shutterstock.com.